Sid and Duck

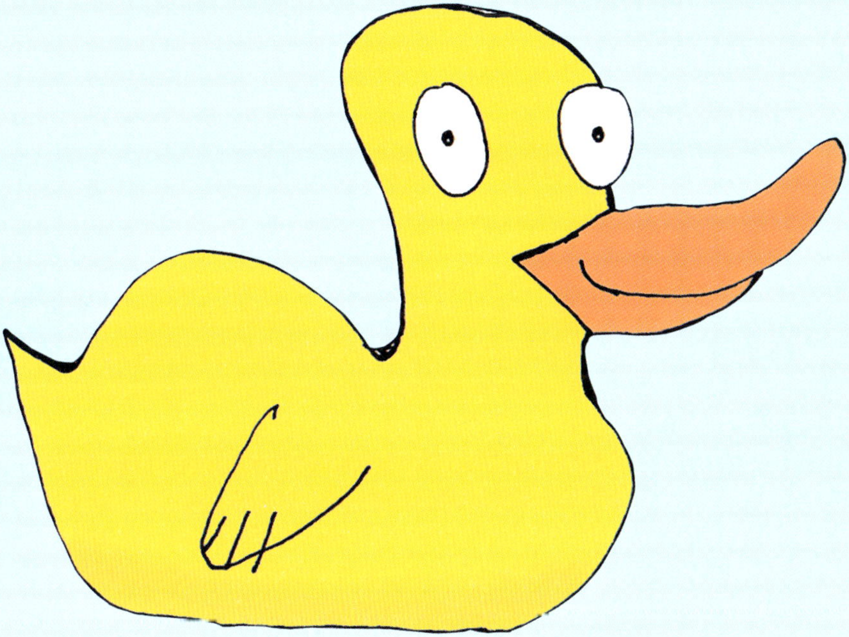

Written by Emma Lynch
Illustrated by Jess Mikhail

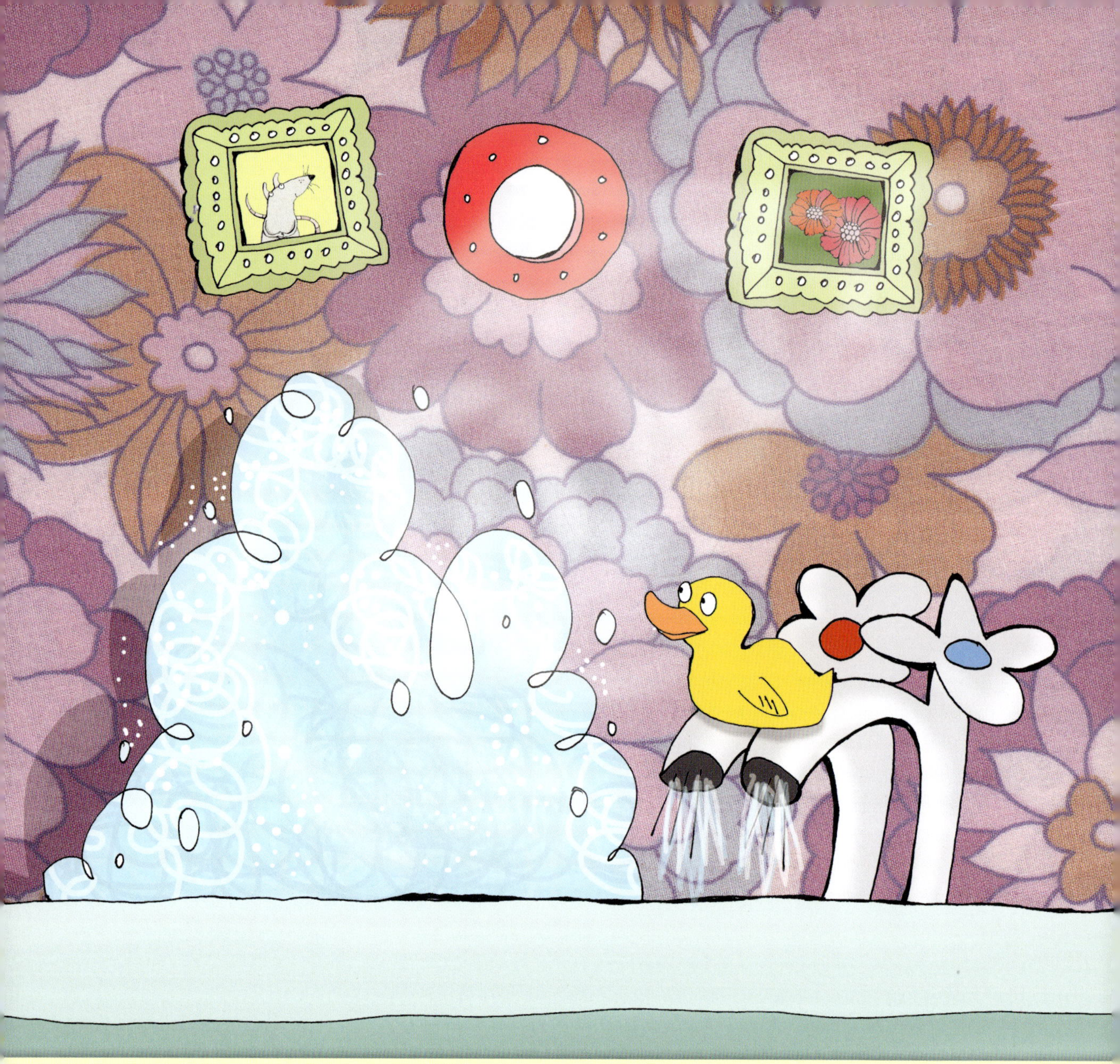

Duck is on the tap.

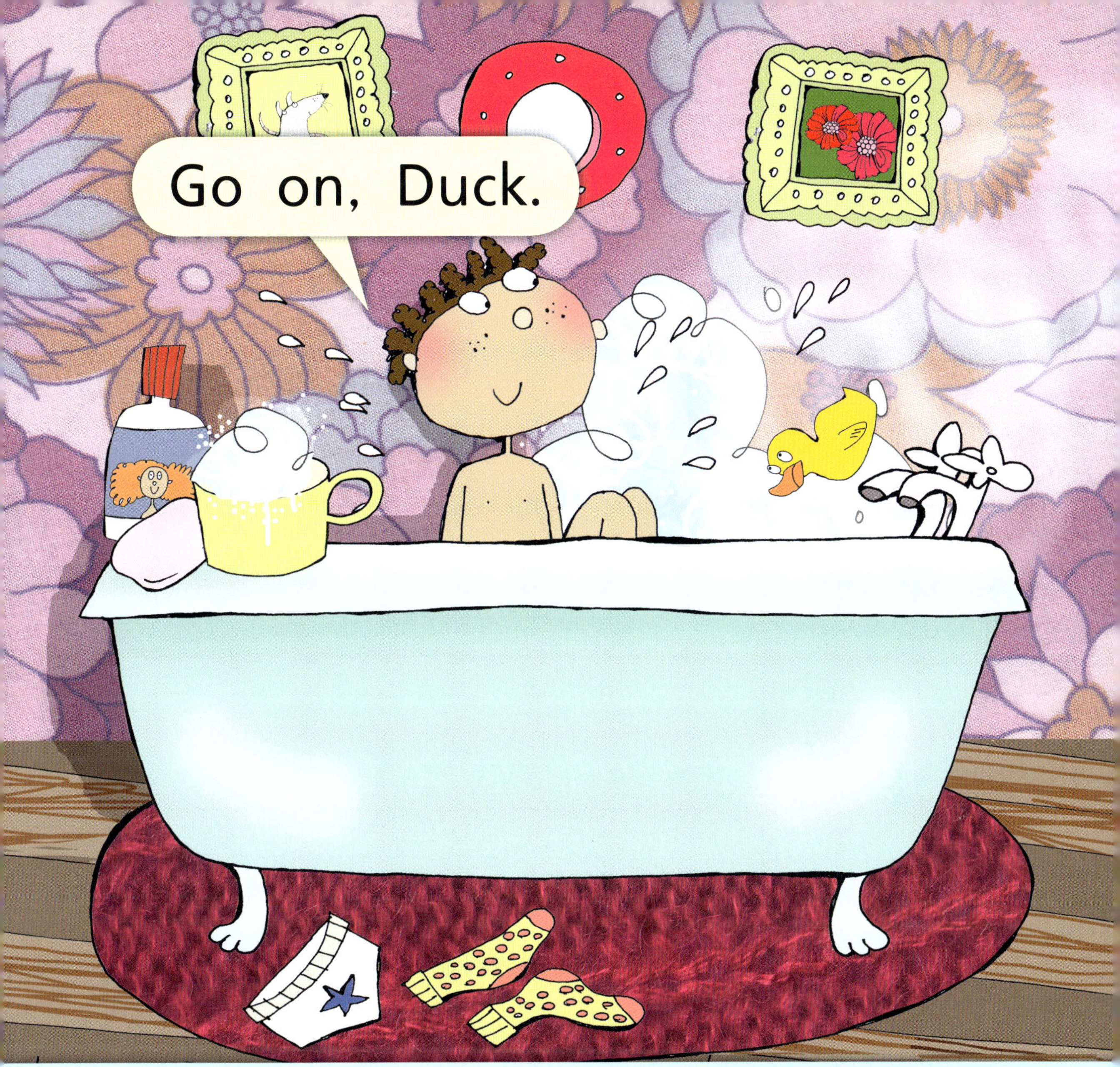

Sid gets in.

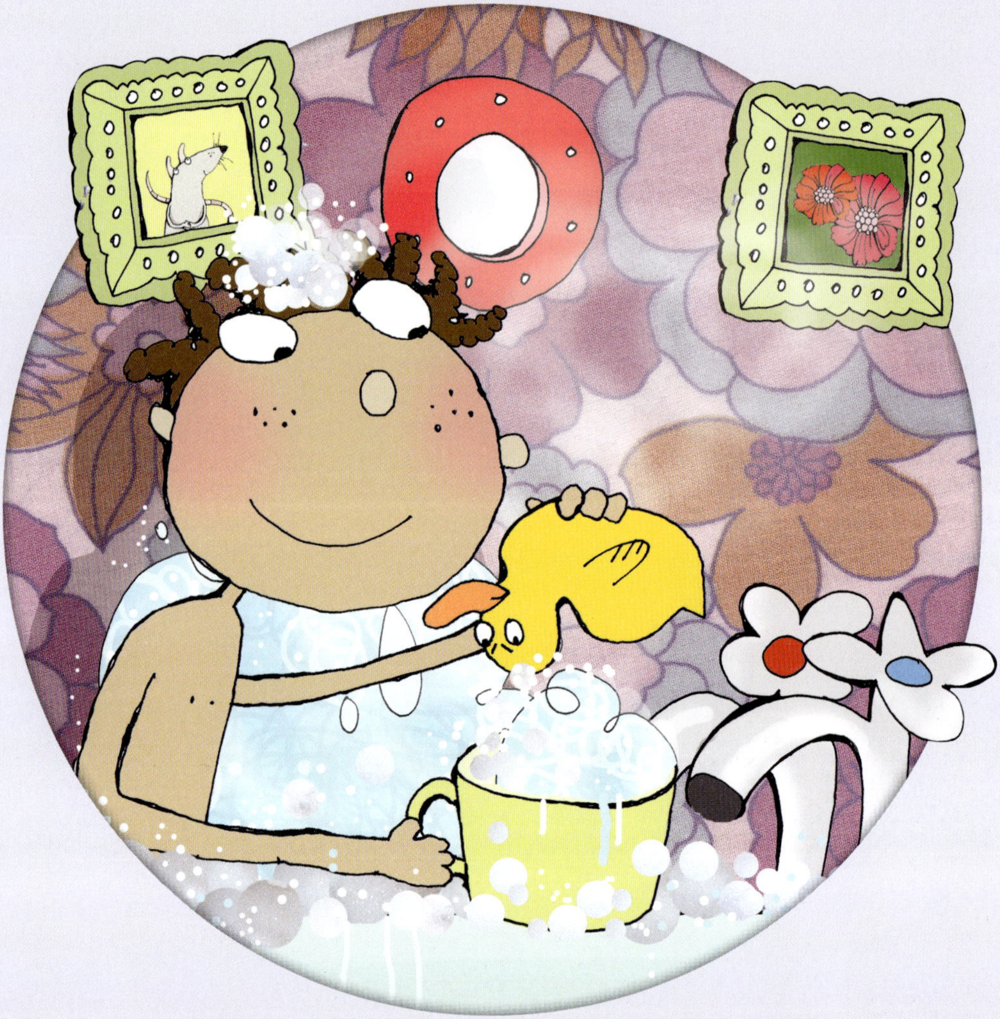

Sid dips Duck.
Sid ducks Duck.

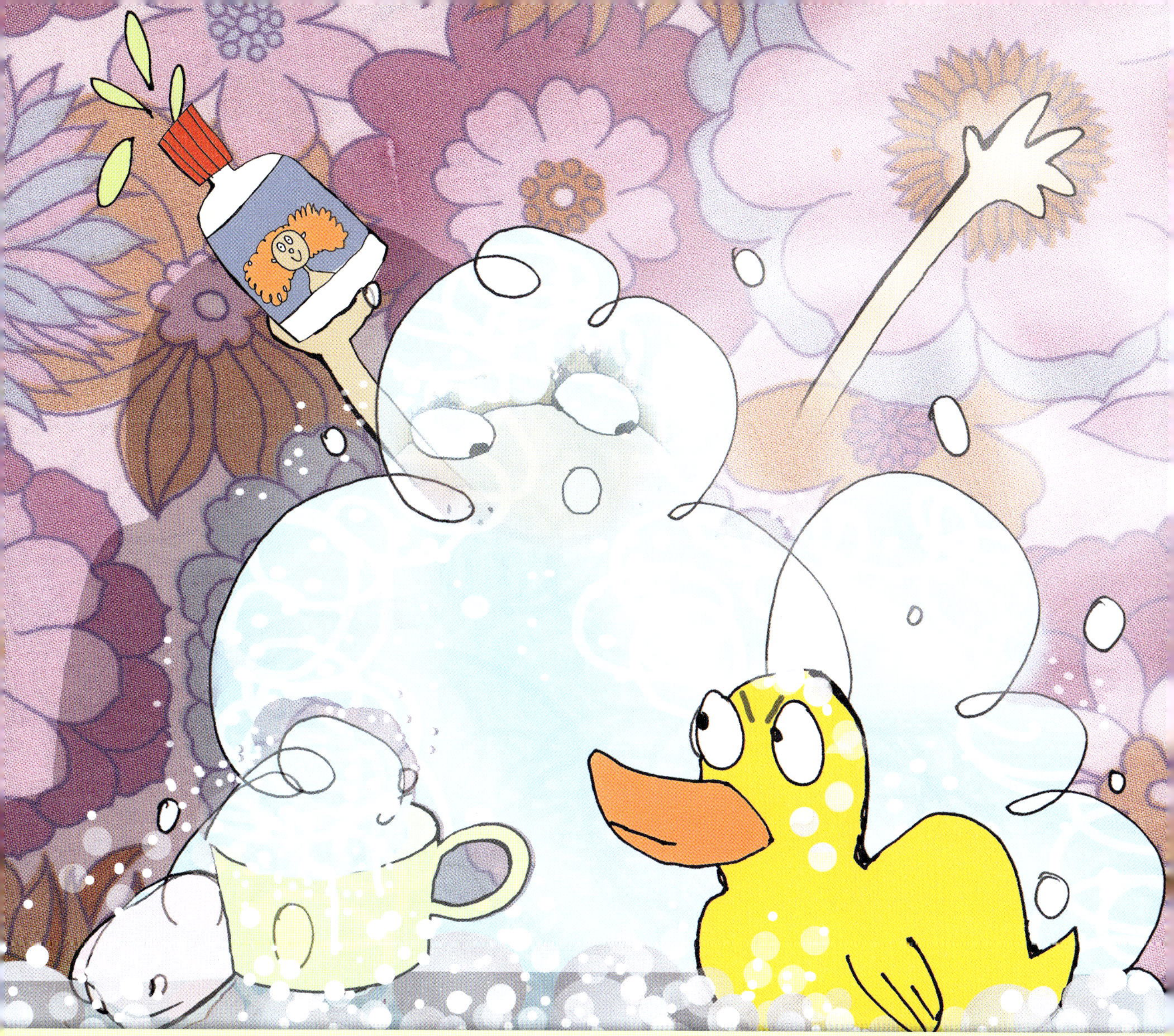

Duck is mad at Sid.

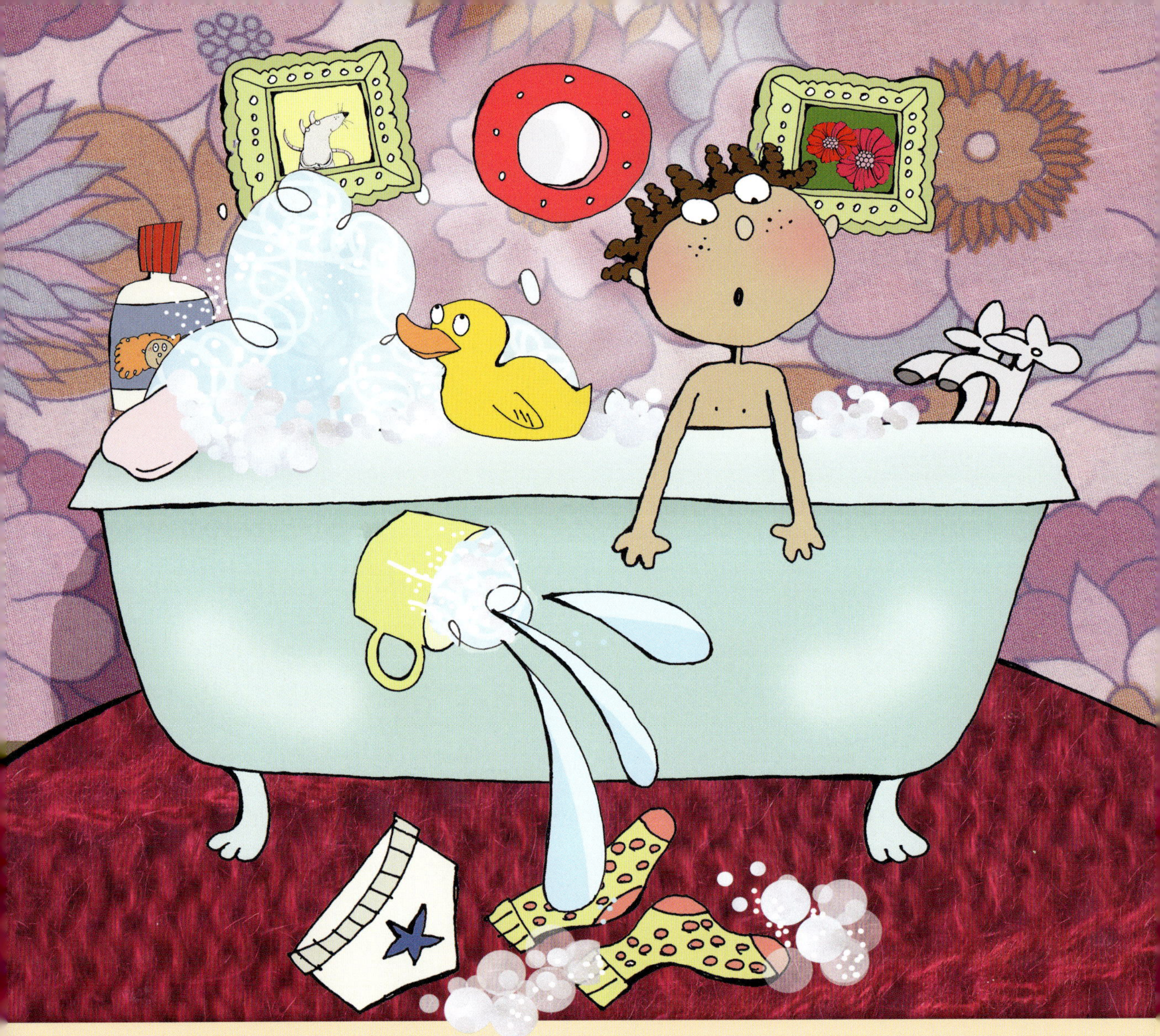

The cup tips up.
Suds go on the rug.

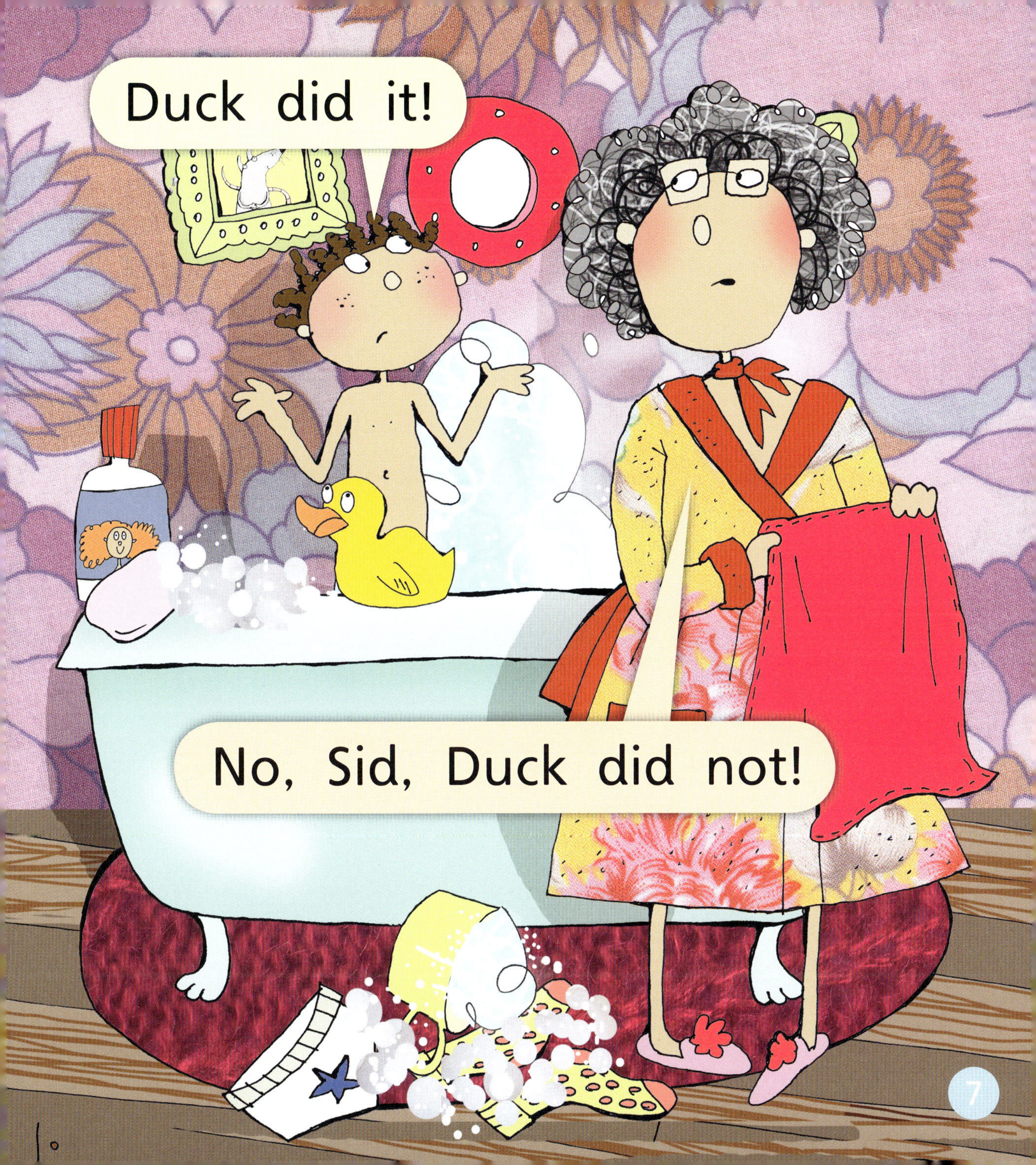
Duck did it!
No, Sid, Duck did not!

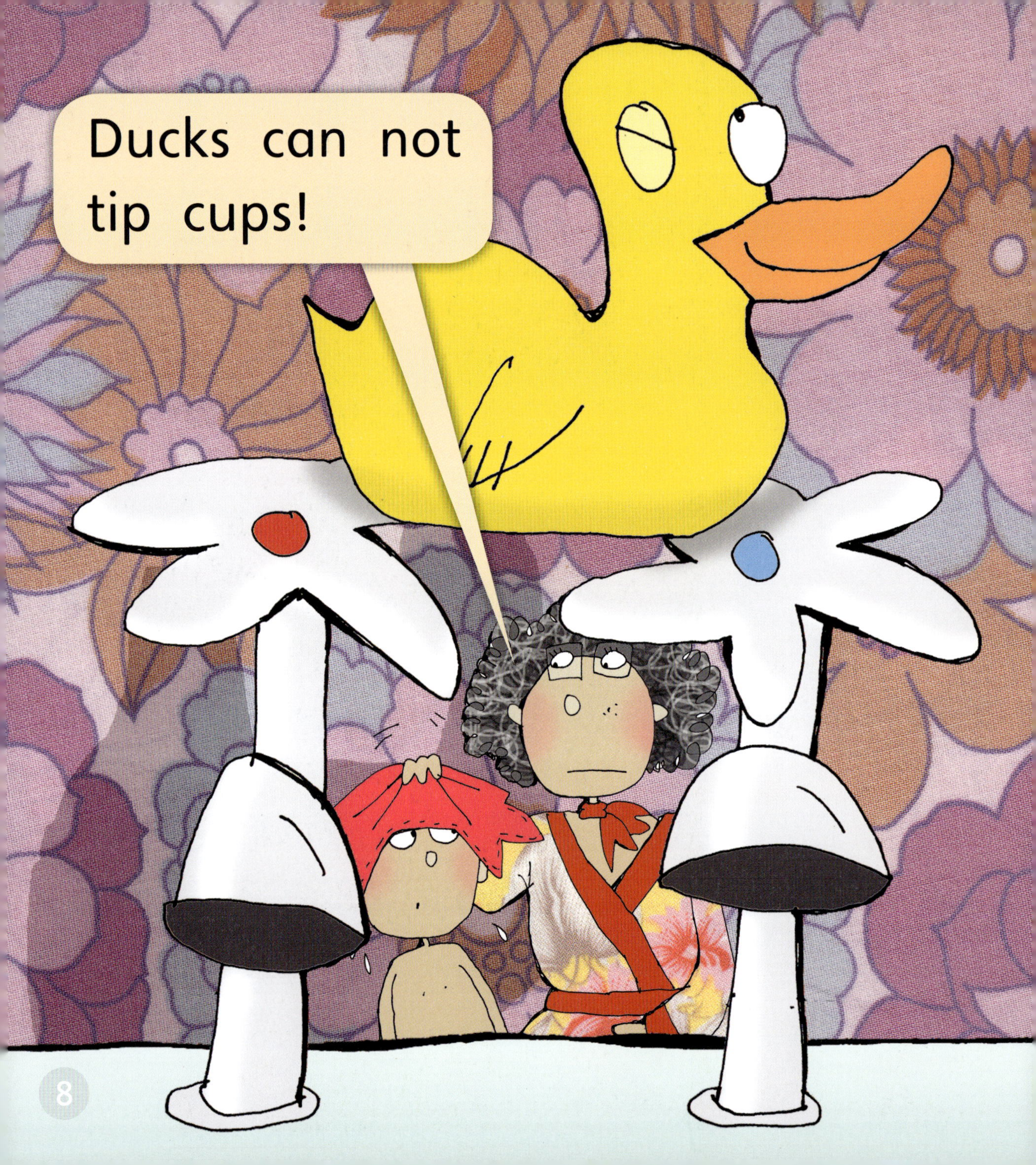
Ducks can not
tip cups!